Cantos from a Small Room

Cantos from a Small Room

Robert Hilles

Wolsak and Wynn . Toronto

Some of these poems have appeared or will appear in: *Antigonish Review, Black Apple, Event, Dandelion, The Fiddlehead, The New Quarterly, Poetry Australia, Poetry Canada Review, Prairie Fire, Prairie Journal of Canadian Literature, Raffia, Secrets From the Orange Couch, White Wall Review, Zymergy.*

The author acknowledges the financial support provided by the Alberta Foundation for the Arts and the Canada Council during the completion of this book.

The publishers gratefully acknowledge support by The Canada Council and The Ontario Arts Council.

Author's Photograph by Norbert Gousseau
Typeset in Palatino, printed in Canada by The Coach House Printing Co., Toronto.

Wolsak and Wynn Publishers Ltd.
Don Mills Post Office Box 316
Don Mills, Ontario, Canada, M3C 2S7

Canadian Cataloguing in Publication Data
Robert Hilles, 1951-
  Cantos from a Small Room
Poems.
ISBN 0-919897-37-1
I. Title.
PS8565.I66C36 1993   C811'.54   C93-093914-X
PR9199.3.H56C36 1993

Fourth Printing

These poems are dedicated to Austin, Rebecca, and Breanne,

to the memory of Roberta Knight
(for Rebecca, Chris, Teresa, and Doug)

and to the memory of Robert Billings

Special thanks to all my friends, especially Claire Harris for her editorial suggestions, and to Ken Rivard, Christopher Wiseman, Barry Dempster, Charles Noble, Allan Safarik, Allan Brown, Monty Reid, Mick Burrs, Richard Stevenson, Bob Stallworthy, Patrick Friesen, Kim Maltman, Roo Borson, and to the students, faculty and staff of the DeVRY Institute of Technology.

CONTENTS

Cantos from a small room

Walking on wild air

CANTOS FROM A SMALL ROOM

(In memory of Roberta Knight 1932-1989)

3658
424- 3568

CANTO 1: SPRING CANTO

It is spring and dead animals are everywhere.
This week they discovered a skull in a city park.
It's spring and in a nearby graveyard
a boy stands his fingers crushing a handful
of flowers his cheeks shining in the sun.
It's spring and the truth ought to be written down
somewhere forged onto paper so that those who
lust after power or strength could read it from
every window they look out. It ought to be something simple
like: "Truth is a whore for everyone" and we could pronounce
our names down narrow streets where history once
was as important as the cheek of a lover on a hot day.
It takes a week to break down the flesh of a man
aged 25 to 40 left in a park his eyes gone.
His skull left to the howling wind until spring.
Horses nest their warm nostrils in the cavity of his skull.
Later dogs carry some of his bones
across fields into the backyards
where children watch as they bury them.
Four policemen and an anthropologist wander through
the dead grass telling stories to one another as spring
begins its brilliant descent. At the back of a bus
a small boy cries and his mother
presses her face against the window and counts the
houses on the street turns away because all day she has
wanted to die has wanted to peel her face from her skull
lie down and not be discovered until spring.
Her hand touches the boy's face
and as she turns around she sees that everyone else
on the bus has their hands hidden in pockets
their mouths are wet from thinking of the dead. She fixes
her eyes on nothing in particular imagines again a field
near the edge of the city and a skull.
Her son trembles in his small mound of blankets.

She thinks of Ezra Pound and the way his teeth shine
in all his pictures and the way his poems find their way
inside her. That man who died comes to her,
his face looking at her from the bus mirror. She turns
to her son and he has stopped crying the bus nearly
empty as she walks to the front she says the word
poetry to the bus driver he looks at her and decides
that she is crazy but he says nothing thinks instead
about spring freeing us as our spirits leave us to whisper
from the mouth of a skull rolling in the grass
blowing across the field while nearby an anthropologist
pauses before stepping into a car.
"I saw Pound out that window," she thinks,
"he was flapping his arms as he smiled from behind a beard."
"Why did he like the number 26?" she asks
not looking at her son not afraid any longer
that the reconstructed skull will come back to suffocate
her with kisses. She knows the hole
the size of a ring finger that it wears near
where its left eye was knows how its white flesh
began to peel in her hand as the baby slept
in the back seat. Was it Pound and his 13th Canto that made
her finally do it. His eyes asking her to repeat
her name. Pound's face beginning to wrinkle as it
lay on her kitchen table. His words singing all
day in her head "To the bath my dear the blinds are down."
The baby carelessly playing with the books she had left
on the floor. Someone answered the phone on the other
end with her voice, her screams broken by the name of a
dead poet found in a field his face on TV his name
the first word of a libretto about death.

So slowly the bus stops today in this new suburb
her face leaving the bus with her perfume the baby
sleeping in his bundle the rest of the bus asleep
their eyes burrowing further and further into a dream
that goes a bit like this.

CANTO 2:   A SIGH A PETAL MAKES

A sigh a petal makes as it falls, she made
and then nothing more. I remember
her words now "I will not grow old except in the
memories of those who have stopped looking for me."
For months she knew it would happen and the
three of us would sit and drink tea and death
joined us and we were shy at first looking
into magazines for the faces of young women.
Still she remained defiant lifting her eyes
as she spoke. I was awkward more awkward than
either of you and I would kiss her
as she left and her warm lips healed my blunders.

There are a lot of words I want to leave out
place blank spaces here and there so that
others will know that there is too much I don't
know that her death fills every corner of my
life and each day I think of her barren form
left for the flames as we walked down the street
numb. Earlier she would visit us bringing roses
and a book she just finished. Some nights
I hold my head in my hands for hours and I feel
as though I am walking down empty streets
while everyone else is asleep. Through it all
the chemotherapy, the hair falling out and growing back,
she would smile, light a cigarette and ask me
about my day as if I was the one who was
dying. Later in that room with the five
on the door she would do the same and then point to
the shelf on the wall where she had placed some toy
for Breanne. As I would turn to reach for it I could
feel her eyes close behind me and I would stand there
unsure that I could make them open again. I tried to say
something, anything that would drag her back into

this room to make her see the pale glory of the light
from outside as it bounced off two grey buildings
to reach here. I remember her at Christmas drinking wine
and once in a while rising so slowly to go to the bathroom.
I listened to her read to Breanne
and from those words and her voice I learned
that each of us faces death alone not able to let
others near enough to grab hold of our passing.
Today Rebecca is over packing her mother's things
and I write this unable to stop her words
from entering into my head as I try to trace
her passing with just a photograph and a keyboard.
It has rained nearly every day since she died.
This morning I awoke and the house was empty
and for a short time I imagined that this body I prepare
for death is younger and passing mirrors I forget that
somewhere behind me a crowd is gathering to break in.

CANTO 3: MORNING CANTO

Spring snow on your
sidewalk is too white as if it were perfected
in the night by an aimless god.
Your wife's mother turns to you
she does not speak for she is dying
and you cannot say a thing.
She sadly rests her hand in yours
and you know that she hears something you can't.

You stop everything in your head for a moment
and hold her hand and listen. She rests.
Her eyes opening and closing
on the hospital bed. You hear her laughing
as a child tying her shoes in the front foyer as her
mother listens to the radio in the kitchen.
She whispers your name but turns towards your wife
and you want to strike at something but there is nothing
left to do. You hold her hand and hope that sometime
it will matter what you did.

Outside the wind moves the trees.
You look out the window to find the rules.
It continues to snow
and everything seems useless. Your hands cool
in your lap and beyond this room you can no longer
imagine anything. Your own flesh is calm.
Her trembling hand lifts
and you see the scars from chemotherapy
and you say "Sleep" three times in your
head but the light still invades the air and
lingers in each of your nostrils.

Today when you hear the water running in the sink
you do not get up to turn it off but listen carefully
as it continues to gurgle.
You know that sight is only partly to do
with opening your eyes. Her
dying eyes opening and shutting all day as she fights
and does not fight as she calls out
a word she has learned in dying.

CANTO 4: SPRING IS A GRADUAL THING

The doctor looked sad this morning
as he visited her still form. He didn't look
at you or anyone else in the room just at her
and listened to her shallow breathing. He left
too quickly dragging what little light there was
with him. He neither paused at the door nor looked back
merely disappeared down the hall as if outside this
room he no longer existed.

There is a spider on the wall and you
do not rise to kill it but watch its
slow ascent to the ceiling and it teaches you
the size of this room and its world no longer
a small place but the vastness of a final breath.
The tap in the other room drips and you go to relieve
yourself again and think of the red bag dangling
from her bed where blood and urine collect.
In the toilet the mirrors seem to sway as you stand above
the toilet bowl, and you feel like you were
being sucked through space at the speed of light
passing this room again and again as your body
continues to pee, and you watch the yellow urine
blend with the clear liquid in the bowl. It forms
the gentle face of a god there. In the mirror
you see the results of a long cold winter
on your face as you move your hand through
your hair feeling for your bald spot.

The spider is on the ceiling now and you can feel
its thousand eyes on you and hear its thin hiss as it
begins to form its web. You know that soon it will
have you cut off from outside its web blocking the
only door in the room. You notice that your hands
have gotten bigger as you hold her one free
hand and feel the faint pulse in her wrist
she does not move but moans now and then.
Sometimes the nurses come in and turn her to
her other side and she calls some muffled word.
Her hand is warm but no longer
able to grasp yours. She is dying and has no
other place to be today but here cut off
from spring and the signs it leaves everywhere.

CANTO 5: DEATH WAITS FOR YOUR SLEEP
TO OPEN ITS ARMS

On the night table she has a tray of flowers
and in her head she can hear a small bird
practice its freedom with a song. She looks
out a window and sees that it's snowing even
though it's April and leaves are bursting
forth on every branch. She can hear footsteps
in the hall and knows it's her son-in-law by
the careful sound of his footsteps. He enters
shyly looking for her small bed in this large room.

She calls him over to her and smiles
and his shyness fades as he catches his reflection
in the window. She talks to him and
he listens and feels the evening light on his face
and knows that he has brought the wrong things
with him. There is nothing he can do but listen
with each breath held in just a little too long.
He watches the IV drip and sees where the veins
have been bruised by the needles.

There is a different rhythm in this room
not one he has felt before.
He can't rest or smile but sits awkwardly in the chair
afraid that if he were comfortable it would make
her death easier. She is calm, hopeful, falling
asleep now and then as they talk and he does not
wake her but waits for those distant blue eyes
to open again to hear her clear voice echo
through the nearly empty room.

He feels as though he were swimming
and there was no shore nothing
but water and beneath it fish waiting softly

for his large weight to sink to them. In the moments
when she rests he looks around the room and notices
the sad beauty of all the flowers people have sent
and he searches for the ones his wife and daughter
picked out and they look like yellow and red ghosts gently
lifting their heads to the ceiling. He wonders what
she thinks when she sees these flowers with their
coloured faces staring at her from everywhere in the room.

When she sleeps she dreams of being in a sky that is neither
blue nor grey her head clear and filled with voices
she remembers voices that whisper just out of hearing
distance. She does not see him when she wakes
but knows that someone is here waiting although
she is uncertain why it is snowing and
there are so many flowers in the room.
Her neck is sore and she reaches for it
but her hand is tethered to the IV and can't reach
the pain. Then she remembers that he has spoken and
she turns to his tired form his face long and narrow
uncomfortable with the sunlight from outside. She doesn't
know what to do how to reach him to uncover the darkness
he is wearing at this moment.

As more and more of her sleep fills with this darkness
they are both powerless to do anything but dream and wake
with memories as wide as the lives they have both just
crossed. After a while she says "You must go the children
are waiting" and he rises obediently and moves to her
and feels her faint breath on his cheek and he walks
backwards to the door watching her slip again into sleep.
Only at the door does he realize he is holding
his hat in his hands and doesn't know what to do with it.

Suddenly he stuffs it into his pocket and leaves,
a nurse turning away from him as he passes his
eyes aimed at the floor.

Alone again she begins to dream but feels someone touch
her hand and the snow outside has stopped and through
her eyelids she can feel the chill lift from the sky.
But she knows there is nothing to plant this spring
that it is too late now and as she sleeps the IV
slowly bleeds into her and she is tethered a little longer
to this large room as white as her face is becoming.

CANTO 6: CANTO FOR A GROTESQUE DANCE

We begin in a house or shack on a street where
other children ride bikes and pretend to be
in some exotic place. On one side of the street
there are willow trees on the other nothing.
At this age we don't believe much but listen
to ourselves die at night and near morning our bodies
begin to engage the world as it
moves through the tender marrow in our bones.
Later we sometimes think that we are what the TV describes
us as plain and graceless as it shows our lives back
to us not like a mirror but thrown asunder planned
by famous people who are not careful enough with
their power. Sometimes we wake with our bodies
on fire and we turn on the radio or stereo
and the voices that come out neither comfort
nor frighten. Some morning we wake up
on a cancer ward and our mother
or father breathes faintly with the aid of oxygen.

At age 37 or 30 we are parents too our children
neatly piled into daycare centres while we hold
these warm hands that greet us each morning
as we visit the cancer ward. We are too young
or too old depending on which door we enter or leave.
On a stairwell we listen to our footsteps and
imagine that someone is following us up or down
in this grey manufactured place. On the fifth or
third floor a janitor mops a hallway and his
teeth sparkle as he swings his mop and as we
pause perhaps we should feel like children again and want
to dance down this damp dangerous place.
Instead we cough into our trembling hands. Before the room,
it might be 585 or 319, we stop, listen as down
the hall a nurse whispers to someone in a wheelchair.

When we enter the room we want to
smash open a window to let the north wind blow
its cold power across the face of the dying.
Still we know the rules and instead
move our lips as though at the point of drowning.
Instead of a mouth full of water or air there is
a lump of numb flesh that was once our tongue.
Suddenly we feel as though we were rolling down
a hill waiting to be stopped by a wall or the
foot of an adult. Eye contact at this moment
is worse than a slap in the face and slowly
we open our hands and lift them over our head
grabbing at the light as though it were on fire.

She speaks from the bed not with her eyes
or mouth but with a gentle nod and a smile.
What keeps bringing us back despite the desperation
and the pain is the hope that outside this room
somewhere a doctor is waiting with the face of a god.
During these many visits and tears we learn
that behind the beauty, the calm preparations,
there is nothing but a quick oblivion.
Sometimes we think of the days
we spent together drinking tea in the sunlight
calmly ignoring the light on our faces.
Each day night comes and with it we lose our power.
We turn off the lights and lie in the dark for an
hour or two while our heads fight off sleep. We hear
the world breathe a counter breath to our own
as we breathe in as it breathes out. Each of us understands
too late that luxury has nothing to do with how bright
our houses are lighted or who comes to the door
it has everything to do with postponing death
one more hour as a son or daughter rushes in from the airport.

On the day that she dies we forget about the weather
about the news about the house insurance.
After that we cry or kiss a loved one over and over.
Later, much later, we climb
a large hill and watch airplanes lunge into the sky
and know that in the centre of one of them
somewhere a hand is raised in a solitary wave.

CANTO 7: THERE ARE NO ACCIDENTS BETWEEN LOVERS

I turned away and did not speak but
listened to your voice waver as
your mother's final breath passed.
We waited all day knowing that it would be
soon tomorrow or the day after but soon
and still it was too quick as if suddenly
a switch had been thrown somewhere.
Both of us wanted her to stand up to walk over
to where we were sitting and put her
arms around us as she has often done
in the past. But we knew that the past
is a fragrance that could not reach into her room.
Looking at her closed eyes I wondered if
where she dreamed there was
a bird singing outside her window.
After she died, I gripped your hand and
saw that in death even music falters.

I can not forget her final breath
that last moment so quiet it
passed unnoticed by everyone there.
We were all talking and did not hear.
We felt helpless and turned to the window
hoping to see her face but there was
nothing but a sky filled with sunset.
The world outside so quiet it was deafening.
I did not know that death would be so quiet
a pause that most alive do not hear
their ears listening too hard for something else.

She did not open her eyes or sit
up suddenly and point at anyone just
stopped breathing. None of her
sweet laughs we used to wake to

when we lived in her house, none
of the wide smiles as she bent
to lift Breanne, her granddaughter.
That is what makes it so hard
the memories that linger even now
months later summer all around us.

Some nights I talk to her as you sleep
and I know that sorrow is a thing
that continues long after the world
has grown up around the absence.
We fill each day as we can forgetting
her phone number or never driving by her house
as we once did to see if she was home.
Staring at her picture in the hall trying
to remember the sound of her voice.
Everyone else in the pictures fades until
all we can see is her staring out
at the camera as if she were in a
foreign country and wasn't
sure of the customs.
Sometimes her name pops into my head
and I say it over and over afraid
I might forget how I would call to her
from the living room at her house as
she knelt outside in the flower bed
planting things I still can't name.

When we speak of her our voices pause.
We know that there is a losing
side to love and even after she is gone
we go on loving her while we learn
to live in new ways waiting at Christmas
for her piano playing even though

her piano is at our house now and
sits silent as if it has forgotten its music.
As I pass it each day in the hall,
I think of our lovemaking and of your
mother alone moving through the thoughts
of so many each day but soundless
faint like her final breath
implanted on so many.
Some nights I stand recklessly in the rain
and feel my life leaving and coming
back to me each moment and as I stare
I see how the world opens around my place in it
like everyone else I am tied not to the sun
or moon or the voices I shape each day
but to this faint breath in my chest
moving softly to my mouth and out
noticeable to you only as I sleep.

CANTO 8: GENTLE SUGGESTIONS

She turns from you to your daughter and smiles
one final time as Breanne holds her hand. For
a moment you think that you hear church bells ringing
and go to the window but your reflection looks withered
in the glass as night has moved in again with a rush.
Why five floors up you wonder, why is this room so small?
You work out its dimensions in your head over and over
each time arriving at new ones not sure why it matters
after all. Holding yourself together by telling stories
that have the odours of lovers at night the musk
from their dreams entering your mouth as you speak.
You don't know why reality doesn't matter any more
as your wife bends to her mother's lips.
The earth is round and fits into your palm
the only place left that you can protect.

Your wife grows in the hospital room doorway
as she leaves. Her mother points
at the window and you understand nothing
that is happening to her. Instead you fumble
with your hat and remember that beauty
was something that you found on a postcard one morning
looking from a shop window and not wanting to turn back
watching the slope of a mountain as if there was a god's
face up there somewhere that you needed to find.

The day of the funeral people come to her house
all day long. Some much older than the last time
you saw them others remarkably the same,
each awkward at the door for a moment their faces
betraying their uncertainty. You try to make sense out of this
but give up after awhile go to the kitchen and fill your
glass with wine. You remember standing in this room
the day she moved in your hand holding a beer as she

moved past you as she does now. Death is bottomless
and those that survive know nothing of it share only
a few words and go to empty rooms to practice their own.
On her bedside table there are half finished books
and you try to close them but they will not. Bent open
for days at the same page they assume that position
like the dead frozen in the posture of their final
breath no longer able to change to move to a sound
or face the sun one final time. Nothing
except a mouth half open the air caught in there
neither expelled nor taken in.

Today you go with your wife to the garden
store and watch others plan their spring with arms
full of seeds and equipment. You think of her mother's
green thumb the way she would rise early on a Saturday
and move through the rows of budding plants bent
all day despite her bad back bent to nurse a weak stock
or lift a plant with gentle suggestion move it slowly
to a new posture. Each of us sleeps a new way every night
opening our eyes even as we dream knowing for a brief moment
the difference between death and life. Somewhere deep inside
poetry washes against something and we are moved.
Strum a guitar late into the night while a child rests
on a lover's lap. Gently, sweetly we go about
our lives know more and more that there are rooms
we pass without entering and days
when the heat drives us to the lake
and nights when a child cannot get settled. It is not
death so much that we race against watch as each we love
prepares for it differently. No it is the smoothness of
another's face their gentle eyes losing their power
even in the light. We see the Milky Way at night and listen
to the Nutcracker Suite while children open presents.

We think of gifts and know the importance
of breaking into our own lives in time
of reaching inside another for just a moment
their tender breath comfortable in our ear.

It is important to move across a room full
of ghosts without being taken in.
Our heads are places where we can hide
safely for a little while. Her face was too smooth
on that last day her skin nearly
transparent on the pillow and you knew that there
was something you had to say but it was not until
much later that you found a way to begin.

CANTO 9: THE DREAM CANTO

Seeing you in your coffin makes me want to
wake you and to make death return another
day when crocuses are not blooming on the
hills behind the house. The bruise on your
hand where the IV rested does not go away even
in death it lingers betraying the undertaker's
careful work. You do not smile or move even
though you would have liked to see the people
here. Instead all we can do is lay flowers and
read poems that slow us down and make us think
of your dust as it moves through a bed of roses
finding rest in the quiet earth. Your lips
are dry your hair softer but combed in a
way you would not have liked.

Each of us before your coffin listens
for a sigh to steal from your lips.
Your new silence does not seem right.
We do nothing but listen deeply to
your life pass through our heads.
We whisper the words you liked the most,
or think of the colours you thought of
when in pain or alone or sad.
We know the shape you formed around each
of us is gone and we look from one to another
like sleepers waking from a long dream.
In this room one of us thinks of the sea
and feels it pound the lava of the beach
then turn again into the sea
falling into its grave of water.

We have brought you flowers because they can
hear you better than we can as they burn with you.

32

Our eyes photograph all this and yet the
ceremony remains invisible.
Quietly, we alternate our fingers in another's grip
and grief does not leave us but takes us like fools out
into the sunlight. It was at sunset that you quietly
stopped breathing and those of us there
took hold of your hand or kissed your lips
as if a part of you could still be reached with such
efforts. We did not sing but wept and nothing passed
to us except the spring day we later poured out into
the sun's final rays blinding us.

We kissed each other because inside
there was nothing but light.
Your voice called softly from the hospital but we
could not hear it any more could not
return to that room even the few minutes away changed
everything. Your body merely a husk now was not something
we could spend the night beside any more.
After days alone with you in that room
looking out towards the mountains and the half block
to your house, we can not go back to you any more.

After the funeral we linger in front of the
funeral home no longer sure how to stand or speak.
We avoid talking about your death coming so soon
in your 57th year. Earlier your daughters
couldn't stop kissing you. Each bent to your brow
slowly awkwardly not the way they would have if you
were still alive. You would have liked that kissing
by each of your daughters just as they were made with
your flesh and love and you held them fresh from your body.

Now they stand before your coffin and know it is not you
that they see. Death completes nothing
and as I bend to your face I see that what you have
left for us is not this shell but the dreams around it.
As I kiss you this last time, there are no eyes
to open to nothing but the smells the undertaker
could not take out and that bruise on your hand where
the IV was for days. You do speak as we part as
you once would have. No all your words are left
here where I stand left folded into notebooks.
Scribbled in your quick hand. They do not tell us
how to bring you back and we are left helpless
reading them to each other to hear again your
voice part the darkness as it once did.

CANTO 10: CANTO FOR THE DEAD

History has two parts one negates the other
and you listen to the hissing.
You are crazy, plump.
A bird laughing by your window means nothing
except that you do not notice the world.
You take a shit or fuck all night but listen
all the time listen to the world hiss and a
snake wrapped around your arm whistles in
your ear with a soft tongue. Everyone has eyes
even the dead who are kind because they can
no longer lie or come to you whispering their
defeat. Ah, this country, this life you say
the mountains in the distance in every direction
except east. You are dragged down by the anticipation
by the quiet lift of a lover's hand. Even in
the middle of the night you crave something
an embrace or a tongue that does not speak but
licks its way into your ear. Crave the daylight
the city view that does not change.

Children pass your house as if they were walking
out of your sleep. You are crazy reading poetry while
in the nude, dreaming at night lines you never
remember in the morning, lines that would have
freed you if you could have grasped their implications.
You are kind to yourself most. Others stand in line
for your affection for your sweet breath.

This is a farewell a beginning that cannot begin.
You wake and want to make love even though it
was fear that woke you. Restless you walk around
your house listening to the radiators.

Does it matter that you are not strong that even
as a child you could not look at death without
being caught in its delicate stare? Does it matter
that your thighs sing in the morning and do not move
but rest beneath the covers?
Your fist is strong but shatters nothing lands
on your own knee. Crazy, you are listening to the world
hiss in the throat of a lover. Listen to the kindness
you have left behind its long dress hanging in a
window down the street. A bird laughs by your window,
as illogical and true as that may sound, you laugh too
walk across the street and tear a daffodil out of the ground.
Softly you begin to tear the skin from your eyes
begin to peel the scales from your tongue.
You are prepared to enter any graveyard and listen.
Death the act of hearing a bird laugh at your window
the blinds hiding its face a tanager or a swallow
it's not important as you look at your hands and smile.

CANTO 11: THE WIND LEAVES WITH US

Some mornings I wake to an opera on the radio
and I think of her hand raised to me
and how small I was as I kissed it and she
smiled and I knew that her defeat was mine too that
there is little that the living can share with the dying.
Her cold small face will be with me for good now
touching me from time to time as I turn to a window
and see snow on an April morning or as I rush to
collect the children from a neighbour and I think
of her calm voice coming from the back seat explaining
the pain as if it was a small beautiful object she
could hold up to the light. I wanted to run my fingers
down her face to find her pulse and feel its faint
drumming on my fingertips instead I sat by the end
of the bed and explained nothing but my anguish.

I begin to heal a bit today and I see
that we can't expect too much from life that half
of it is magic and the other half terror.
As I mow the lawn I feel the earth vibrate but I know
it is only my knees and I look behind me for the first
time and feel someone's breath. I play with Breanne
and she invents stories I can't keep up with.
She quietly passes my room several times before
entering and I remember when I used to do that as a child
and I am frightened. Today we pretend to be mother and son
and I listened as she instructs me on the phone and I follow
her commands and I feel free for the first time in my life.
We begin to dance together moving our bodies to
an unheard music. We collapse on the couch laughing so hard
I nearly pee and I know that some day this will matter even
a lot more than it does now. Roberta moves to the couch too
even though Breanne does not see her and I am amazed
by the many forms that our learning takes.

Earlier in her coffin there was nothing no screaming no
struggle nothing except the music and words that the living
brought numbed by the gentle ceremony we were performing.
Together we all left for a small supper not sure why
we felt such a sudden need to fill our stomachs.

CANTO 12: WHERE SPRING CANNOT REACH

From the fifth floor I feel
as if I am in a tower watching a ruined world
put itself back together.
Each time I look down to the street below
I can see two lovers turn to kiss but
from this height I can't hear anything
except a slow breathing behind me.
I stop thinking about what might be and
listen instead to the breathing listen
and practice as the sky bulges with stars.

Why isn't it winter I ask as I feel for
the banister in the dark. Descending to the kitchen
I feel her loss break open my stomach but
instead of wailing I tumble onto the floor
and tuck my head into a hood of hands.
I could sing for her today move my hands
across the spines of books she left for me.
I keep remembering her last time in our house
the trouble she had making it upstairs and
yet she smiled as I passed the room where she
was lying down. I said nothing then just
smiled back and felt as though I were living
a thousand lives at once. Rebecca torn between
seeing and not seeing her mother's slow ascent
while Breanne celebrated her fourth birthday below.
Each of us goes on for different reasons walks
away from the mirror in the morning astonished by
different things. Each of us surrenders a different
way moving through a dream as if followed by
the ghost of a parent. In death we are neither
naked nor calm and the white secret of our bones
flows like milk through our veins.

Today I can still hear her voice as I sit alone
and I remember the places inside that belong to her.
The chairs in the room claim their own music
as I wait for what I don't know. Perhaps
there is nothing the living can do but begin.
Endings are around us all the time our lives
the slowing down of our hearts. I open a window
and there is not a sound as though a long piece
of music had just ended. Nothing is retained
from this moment except for the few words I record
on the page. Even they are dark and small and do
not resemble the intent that chose them.

I still think of her final day the one where I rushed
across town with my car windows wide open listening
to church bells. I felt calm but uncertain
as if winter might never leave this year.
When I arrived at her room she seemed so quiet
as though death was just a pleasant afternoon nap.
Only after she died did spring begin to
reach its hands into my life and as we plant
the annuals in the front bed I think of her
mouth half open in death and I know I can't
face this fall as the bare skeletons of these
plants will wait patiently to be buried in snow.

The wind is an old companion as I sit in the back
yard and listen for its approach. I fold my hands
and begin to pray not to any god but
to her pale face before me not yet fading but
waiting in dreams to find new shapes.

I don't use words or thoughts just the wind's
delicate voice moving far down into my throat
and filling my lungs with regret. I will remember
the dignity of her hands as they lay on sheets.
For a moment they closed as if around a bouquet
of flowers and I smiled then not sure why
and I moved slowly away as if neither of us
belonged any longer in the hospital room.

It is nearly summer but it is still
winter and I can't say what I want to say
hiding each night beneath blankets and waiting
for the soft breath of winter on my cheek.
She will not remember the last flowers
we brought to her or the others that arrived
each morning as she slept but I will.
I am silenced by the way they smelled and
how they exploded so gently into full flower.
Some night I will know that her dying was
not as important as all the years that spring
came early and she was out planting the hardy
stocks in April singing a song that escapes me now.
It is lost with all the others she sang
even though each night
I listen for them to rise above
the sullen wind.

WALKING ON WILD AIR

SO

All your mother's pictures on our walls
have changed but I can't say how.
Perhaps they have stopped
seeing us or stopped protecting us
from the full impact of light around them.
Near one I can hear her sigh
as though she had just paused at the top
of our stairs after a difficult ascent.
When she visits her glasses sparkle
whenever she turns her head and I find
it hard to see her eyes.

You hang more pictures find new spots
I wouldn't have thought of to place them.
Your hands tremble across my face and I
wish for a moment that I could share your pain,
the growing grief you hold inside.
Your mother's cancer takes the air out of our lives
and I know what bravery is for the first time
as I watch her play with Breanne.
From the kitchen I can feel you descend
the stairs your steps heavier than
I have ever heard them.
I look out a window where the world is
spinning faster. Some stars are so low on the
horizon that they might be in a neighbour's window.

Death is swelling around everything
and as the afternoon light spreads across the
furniture I imagine Breanne one morning standing
at the door wondering where we are. On her face
the light is timid as though with
a sudden blink of her eyes she could bring
total darkness. She moves through the door
to the outside and carries with her a pain

that starts at her throat and moves down.
From the top of the stairs just out of view
I listen to the door shut. I dig my hands
deeper into my pockets as if searching for
a good place to leave them. All night her
car is parked in front of the house
with the lights on. The dog next door
barks now and then. I am bothered all night
by the shape of my hands. I see them
break things until our bedroom lies in ruin.

When I call out to you in my sleep, you are downstairs
crying. Your eyes show it in the morning.
At the breakfast table I am too serious,
can't see the humour in Breanne's
three year old antics. Instead the cereal in my
bowl looks like the remains of yesterday's breakfast.
You do not speak and I know that love is more
than the habits our bodies assume for us.
Your mother's illness makes me want to go back
to moments when we were deathless.
Breanne won't let me. Her hands in her food search.

I pray for a knock on the door for anything
to make us get up from the table full
not looking out the window or worrying
at all about the time of day. When the phone
rings I know it is your mother because your voice
is full of the familiar HI you use when it is
someone you love on the phone. I try not to
listen but I do afraid the news will be even worse
than we thought. Instead I hear Breanne close her
bedroom door upstairs. When I go up she is talking
to her toys and as I eavesdrop I forget for awhile
what the rest of my life will be like.

MAP OF LIGHT

We begin the journey the same, travellers
hurled together at great speed. Impacting
on a single point of light.
We exist because there is a certain tension
between particles, because somewhere
a blue light is twisted into red, because
at an intersection four cars stop simultaneously.
The radio drums in our ears like the confused
beating of a raven's wings. The light is green
through the window this morning and I try to
lift your face above me but in your eyes
the light is red. What are those bells you ask
and I listen but there is nothing except a
clock ticking and the cat downstairs somewhere
skinning a mouse. There are stars in your eyes
and I move closer to count them. We have accepted
the convenience of our bodies and have learned
how they can fill with passion. The children
we form are part of our shared breath, part
of the moon through the skylight.

Today we put up the Christmas tree and the ornaments
we unpack add shape to the past we carry inside.
We can't find the angel somehow it got lost
when we moved, instead we buy a new one.
I find your mouth over me warming the air
with your breath. You move slowly searching
for a way inside my head, to reach the places
where the light is taken over by night.
Inside me there you dance as though my darkness
formed the sweetest music. As I close
my eyes I can follow your movements hear
your dance far inside me and for hours
later I can not let the light out

can not stop feeling your movements.
You need no map to find the light in me.
I wish we could fold back the darkness
for good, stop our faces from being defeated
by the light, by the days we sit alone
afraid of the mirror, afraid of the way
our faces are wearing out.
We make love at night listen as a train
passes and we feel as though we were on it.

We fit together, not sure why or how
we only know that we do. No one is singing
as we turn out the lights for sleep.
Above us the moon waits as though
it could feel our longing. I turn to you
our lips meeting softly in the dark.
We are wrapped within again. Loving
the quiet, the softness of one another.
Later as you sleep I think of the thousand
different ways we could have arrived at this
moment. I am amazed that we fit as we do,
the light in this room is always white
clear as though here at the top of our house
we have found an atmosphere that lets our longings open.
Light searching inside for the darkness
that has been there the longest.

NOISES OUTSIDE YOUR WINDOW

You wake or fall asleep what does it matter
It is easy to pretend, to lift your eyes
at the last second, breathe slowly against
the cold of a mirror. Face your life
as though it were just noise outside your window.
A child is trapped in a well for two days,
and news of that is beamed in thin strips of light
to anyone passing a humming tv set.
All of us afraid to turn away afraid
that the news is our lives.

When you wake your hands are empty but tired
as though they have held something tightly all night.
Your daughter coughs and you forget everything
that you have been sorting out in half wake logic.
You want to bring the morning to her in a kiss
Listen as she tells you the story of her toys
how they have fallen or are lost or are in love
with one another, as much drama as she can
imagine from her three years.

There is a spot in your brain that you can't control
that ignites when you are shopping or stuck in traffic
or listening to the radio. It is what you have inherited,
and passed on again your body agent to unknown phantoms.
That part of your brain does not sleep but projects dreams
for you all night. Your daughter stands
so powerful at the top
of the stairs her terror short-lived
lost in the cradle of your hug.
The halls in your house are narrow
ceilings so high they are nearly out of sight.
In it you sometimes feel like a seed about
to burst open. Clinging to the air it is still

possible to drown. What saves you is
your daughters anxious cries her sleep as restless
as yours. Dreams invaded by the subtle
pressure of the room's air. In the morning
seeing the last lights fade in the city,
you know the power too, know the consequences
of holding your breath all night.

MARRIED TO IT

The light does not reach the sink in front of you
as you do the dishes and think of your mother
all those nights alone washing dishes
trying to guess the meaning of things.
Her face was a glowing oval in the window.
Her eyes hidden. The earth trying to form
night in her mouth.

Soon you will go out and look
at the stars with your daughter and
see with her how each star is
fixed in space like we are fixed
inside moving only our bodies as we walk.
The earth, married to us, follows and we
feel in control of the whole damn thing.
You want to take your daughter to the place
where stooping you discovered the fullness of
blueberries their delicate skin bruised
in the picking. The blueberry hills are
covered with houses and roads now
and the only plants your daughter would find
are weeds you can no longer even name.

Your daughter kicks at your leg and you
turn to her expecting to see her smiling
but she is looking again at the stars
and holding her hat gingerly on her head.
As she speaks you know that in your mind
somewhere you are still picking blueberries
tasting your mother's pie listening
as a man plays a guitar and does not look
at you. Watching your daughter, you think
you can hear her heart forming a shape
she has learned from stars.
She stands now catching the moonlight
in her wide open mouth.

BLESSINGS

My new son wakes me at 2 AM
and I feel myself waking in another house,
my fingers another's fingers.
I lift my son from the crib
and he smiles sticks out his tongue.
We face one another
and neither squirms nor speaks but
each listens as the rain sounds like an older
child's breathing. I embrace him and
then change his diaper. I linger
for a moment before he goes back to sleep,
and I speak softly to him
stories that I heard when I was his age
stories that are not the same now.
I know he listens with a mind that
appreciates the emptiness of morning.
He puts his thumb in his mouth and falls asleep.

Then I crawl back to bed and put my
mouth on your back and wait as
you fill your mouth with air.
As I move my lips over your back,
you continue to sleep.
Later in the morning you ask me
if Austin woke during the night
and I answer by putting my
face to the cold glass of a window
as if my face were burning.

You, my son, place your
shadow against an empty part of the yard
and listen not to me or to the wind
but to a sound neither deathless nor death.
I am pleased and see the blessings
are numerous. The lives we form
are bigger than a sentence or a poem.
We gage ourselves against the sky.
I teach you nothing.
An old fool, I no longer finish my sentences.
What I am will not last in your warm breath
but fades. The stories I have told
you will last longer my lips pausing
for a moment on your cheek.

LAUGHTER

Our month old son sleeps moving now and then as if
tempted by something new in the world. Some nights
I watch him sleep aware that at some level I do not
exist. It has been a hard spring filled with death
and birth and you climb the stairs at night differently
as if no longer caring how your body wears down by nightfall.

Austin breathes slowly and does not notice the moon or
sun but looks only at my face as he lunges for his
bottle. Some days I wake before his morning feeding and
wait for his cries, wait at the foot of the stairs
listening to the world as it sounded before I was born.
My parents sleep in the guest bedroom and I know that
once they must have felt like this too. I never stop
finding places in my body where I have never felt the
light before. Small tumours the moon has started inside me.

Children help us to see how we emerge into this world
screaming and wondering in our new blue form why nature
could insist on such things. I whisper to my son not
sure if my affection is enough at night gas lodged
somewhere in his gut refusing to come out. I know he
will not remember any of this but will rely on my frail
image of it one evening when the two of us talk about the past.

I think of my mother sitting up at night
talking to god. I move across an empty room to her
and touch her forehead. I am someone who grew inside
her and claimed for her a new part of the world.
On Sundays I take her to a church and wait outside
holding my new son. I ignore gods and churches ignore
the promises they make. My son and daughter sit quietly
in the car as my mother walks slowly to it smiling
faintly. I hold her hand as she gets in and I feel
my daughter's breath at my neck. It isn't until much
later that I will begin to hear that voice from far away.

THIS ONE SHORT POEM

Our son climbs the stairs
and as he nears the top I
can feel the earth try to pull him back
but he ignores it and continues
up to his room. He has taught me
how the poem is a cold thing left
to warm a colder page.
I take all the unfinished ones
to his room to show him but he
does not care sitting on the floor
holding a stuffed animal. The world for
him is complete because it is left
mostly undescribed. He knows that
his father passes his room with a head
full of poems as if it were important
to describe the rooms
where his son learns to be wrong.

Our son sleeps and I wait for his latest
illness to pass. I finger his clothes as if
they were the people he will meet later
in life. I stand near his escaping breath
listening, hoping that it will tell
me what he feels towards me.
Later I speak to him as he eats
his breakfast and I hear my father
whistling outside and know that
our son will remember nothing
of this. I can't forge his place.
His circling hands show
me how his desires come to him.

I have grown into the earth and have found
the roots there that I want
to take an axe to but can't.
Standing frozen in the front yard
I feel the city change around me
as our son and daughter make a snowman.
As they laugh, I see that
everything they know is in spite of me.
I remember my father
standing in the door of his small house
watching me cross a field of snow
after a rabbit. Then suddenly he
disappeared inside my mother'calling
in a voice only he could hear.
Each of us becomes the other,
and life is our only chance to shape
the molten forms surrendered to us at birth.
It is me who takes a few words
and stretches them across a page
hoping that with this one short poem
lives can be mended or saved.

LOOKING BACK

Love is a pale thing until upon
looking back I can see its real shade
a delicate red like the worn
flesh near the eye. I can not persuade
you to stop looking back expecting a crack
to appear in what we have left behind
as if everything is in ruin except what
we steal for the moment from the wind.

MAYBE AND ALWAYS

We are betrayed
by other words stronger words
that make us expect that somewhere
a god waits to take our lives.

Once more we embrace and try to forget
our new son alone grabbing
at the sheet as though it were the hand of a god.
Maybe I will stand beside the bed
and watch a car parking down the street
and you will pull me into bed
your hair in my face teaching me
to close my eyes as I fall.
We share these lives and never expect
"always" to happen expect instead
each morning will show us a new way
to weave our bodies together.

Our lungs have formed other lungs
our eyes have learned sight from our children.
They wait for us in the morning sitting
on the floor their hands caught in their hair.
We understand nothing folding to the pressure
in the air. Our children will ask us how they
should live we'll have no answer now.
They follow us in the dark to their beds
and we can't part the darkness or lift
it from their lives we merely place
a mirror in their rooms and hope
they get the right idea.

On some street where we have lived
apple blossoms come early this spring
and we hear them sing
as we move softly through each room.
Our lives continue to stretch before

us like one long night
of lovemaking our bodies
held by the fragrances we invent
together. Our tongues taste the world
from above and below and find
for us a joy that shapes the short
time we have left.
Our daughter asks about the empty
picture frames we never seem to fill
and we can't explain to her why
we have learned the value of Maybe
and Always two ways of saying I love you
two ways we never use but
continue to obey each hour we are alive.

Every spring there are birds
that come to our windows and
we take no notice.
Our love has never been fascinated
by such coincidences.
Instead we leave a flower on a desk
or near a pillow hide our eyes
from the light as we wake embracing
as if falling through the sky
at a 1000 miles an hour.
We have learned to put aside the magic
in the blood to listen in darkness
as a son or daughter cries
downstairs. We are never hollow
or alone filled by various things
that pass through us each day.
As I undress your eyes open for me
and I see through them a window
I wait at like a bird
a window no one else has ever found.

COMBS

You comb your hair and
this dark room is filled
with splashes of static.
My body is shaped
by your hair and I listen
as you sigh into the mirror
and escape in it to another room
one larger than this where
the moonlight strips the sheets
from the bed and children whisper
their fears at the door.
My hands tremble as
they reach across to you
feeling your soft tongue moisten
them. Our bodies continue
to praise each other even as we
sleep our lives equipped with
different dreams and it is dangerous
to anticipate another's plummet
into the world alone.

The earth is a body too and
we can feel it fall beneath us
and spin. Our lovemaking
fuelled by the attraction of the moon.
Along some river we walk and discuss
our lives together
talk about how our voices
shape a mirror for the moon.
You throw a stone into the water
and we watch it sink as if
beneath the surface somewhere
a god was waiting for such a gift.

In our lifetime we will feel
our bodies burn out hear
our children ascend a final step
to our door entering with tear
laden faces to claim our final breaths.

We will think then of this day
along the river knowing that
as my hand held yours a certain spark
began that no wind could put out.
Near the water a squirrel sits
and we pretend that it waits for us
bearing a message from nature.
A warning we never heed because
we are so preoccupied with
finding our own way out.
We held hands then as we do now
delicately passing a warmth from
hand to hand saying nothing as
the wind passes our door and
lets us sleep another night
without interruption.

We are made and unmade by
time moving into new embraces
wondering how our lives
arrive complete in our heads
memories we don't want
taking us back for hours to
a house where we learned the colour
of darkness. We pass each night
protected by a thin disguise
of rain that fills the fields
as we sleep. Our children

play in their sleep and
once in a while they cough
as if calling their own death.
I make it up the final
steps up to your arms not tired
but possessed by a death that waits there.

Forgive these awkward hands as they
sometimes linger in the night while you
sleep they are powered by a small mind
one that has not yet taught itself.
Sometimes you push me away
and I am glad because I fall asleep then
thinking of you combing your hair and me listening
as you sing what my lips form on your neck
and we fall onto the bed our
lips planting blossoms everywhere.

WALKING ON WILD AIR

He moves slowly towards me and then stops. Neither
friend nor enemy just someone who waits for me to
cough at night who watches my son barely days
old sleep. My father ignores my eyes ignores my
words as they fall around him. I open and close a
door. He does not turn around, does not
notice when I am crazy near losing control of
everything, lifting my hand as if to break a
skull. He lights a cigarette and looks out a
window memorizing the sun laughing now and then as
I walk past nervous with each step.

One of us is crazy and we know it but neither
listens to the rain as it tries to tear the roof
off. Neither of us reaches for a hand to get
up from a chair. We listen to news as if
framed in it somewhere was a voice or message we
could take with us to the grave. Sometimes he
stays awake all night finds a new star in the
heavens. His boyish face greets me each morning at
the table and I look away listen as his forced
breath chimes with the sunlight. His tongue is
black as he opens his mouth to swallow a drink of
beer. I watch his fist open and close. I see
not defeat or longing but the glory of a man
who lives inside his life as if it were the only
place he could be.

I start to recite a poem I
once wrote and he smiles lifts his grandson out of
his crib and begins a jig, a gentle sleek jig,
that takes his feet higher and higher into the
air. He and I were born on the same day have lived
the same lives ending our nights in the arms of a
lover moving our mouths deeper into the unknown.

But we talk more like strangers than friends sit
across from each other and aim our words out a
nearby window.

Some mornings I find him doing push-ups on my front
lawn. I smile not sure why listen as his chest
expands with the shallow grip of a drowning man.
He waits until I go back inside before he stops.
In the kitchen I warm another
bottle wait for him to come inside. I hold
Austin as my father must have held me once long ago.
I listen, for what I don't know, but I listen all
day as if only my ears could discover the meaning.
Noisily Austin sucks the milk from the bottle and
as he does I remember somewhere in this house my
father is dying I sit in a hard chair knowing
that I will recall too late what matters most that
he is already beginning to take off his last
shirt. My hands tremble as they hold Austin's
bottle and the baby knows I can no longer
watch him my head filled with a pounding
that won't let up as if my father was knocking at
the door pleading with me to wake up to watch him
hold the sunlight in his mouth one more time.

ROADKILL

On the road from Winnipeg to
Kenora, we came upon a
roadkill dressed in ravens.
As we approached, the whole flock
formed one bird the shape of death
and moved gracefully into the sky.
We passed over the place quickly
as if it could be forgotten.
Nothing more than a red spot on the highway
vanishing in the rearview mirror.
But the ravens returned swiftly to
finish their business, landing
gently one after another
a sudden black rain.

My father says "Probably a deer."
"But there's hardly anything left," I say.
"A flock of ravens can devour a deer in minutes,"
he says. I want to turn back then
to stop and wait for the pavement around
me to cool. But all I remember is the small
red stain spreading across the pavement.

Nothing left but to drive on
my past left
behind for good, left on the road
for others to pass over
forgotten within minutes.
I needed to find the place inside me
where memories start. It is
near where the breathing begins
but is separate and contains
nothing but waiting.

In Kenora my father talks
to old friends that pass on the street
and I feel invisible. I know no one here
any more. I never lived here, even
though I spent 18 years memorizing its
streets as if sometime later I might
forget how I was formed by them.
Now I lose my way the landscape unfamiliar.

Still these streets are my streets and
my father's we each claim something
different, not a place or land or even a face
but a dream perhaps or a conversation
or even just a sentence.
Our claim so small that the world ignores it
and we move on, not towards or away but
against a world we never see
but bump against day after day.
Late at night I climb the stairs
to check on Breanne's breathing and I remember
Kenora, the town I once knew.
The one I see when I close
my eyes, empty not a soul on the streets
all the houses dark, and as I hold my
breath and watch I see a figure standing
by a car. He listens as I whisper the name
he gave me long ago and my father moves
towards me with outstretched hands.
Finally I know what place this is and why
we come to visit, not because it is ours
or even because we created it with our memories
but because some night long ago we dreamed this.

We went back to Winnipeg the same day
and I listened for angels as I drove.
I remember Kenora because I was born there
and yet I cannot say what it is I remember.
A landscape that always changes perhaps
or a few faces that appear on my tongue suddenly.
I know my father and I see different towns
even as we stand on the same street
waiting for different people to pass. I am never
his son he is never my father. We speak
to one another but never understand
what the words have to do with it
or why, seeing those ravens ascend
into the sky, we were both thinking
of our own deaths on this trip.
In the dark the headlights aimed
at the highway like a set of mechanical
eyes giving out light rather than taking it in.

DREAM

A boy made an appointment with God and waited for him in a
church. After a few hours he knew that God wasn't coming and
he learned for the first time that a god must never reveal
himself even to the faithful. At first, the boy was hurt
by this and stopped reading his Bible and stopped going to
church. He began to have strange dreams at night of walking
through the bush with a pack of wolves. In his one hand he
carried the tail of a deer in the other a rifle. Even though
he walked on two feet and carried a rifle he knew that he
was a wolf and that the leader of the pack was his father.
In a clearing they found a vast lake and on the far shore
stood an enormous moose. As he aimed his rifle his father
spoke in his wolf voice saying: "You can not shoot that
moose because he is all that is left of a once powerful God.
Instead you must climb onto his back and whisper into his
ear the cries your mother made when you were born. Then he
will recognize that you are his grandson." The boy did not
listen to his father and shot the moose instead in an
instant the lake was filled with blood. The wolves all fled
and he was left to drown in the blood. Sometimes he wakes
before he pulls the trigger other times he wakes as he tries
to swim in all that blood. Each time he wakes he knows that
God is trying to tell him something with that dream but he
is too simple to really understand. Instead he goes back to
church knowing that later a different dream will come.

EVEN THE SUNLIGHT IS DANGEROUS

Each day I find the sunlight in the same place on my bed as
I wake for work. Shaving I think of my father shaving
without a mirror always missing a spot here and there and
not giving a damn. As I shave, I think too of my wife still
asleep in a heap of covers her body warm in the places where
we touched. Her back has started to curl a little with age
and she has difficulty lifting the children from their beds.
My friends at work are all married too but we do not talk
about that. Today I feel awful from too much drinking last
night and want to phone in sick but can't. Yesterday the
foreman found me puking into a sink and got mad. Some nights I
dream of being at work. Thousands of loaves of bread
go past me just like at work when I wake up I don't know
if its time to go to work or if I just lay down.

Sometimes I think that I would be happy if I were a doctor,
lawyer, or even manager of this damn bread plant. But other
times I'm not so sure. It's not the money or power that I
want it's just the respect. Like to go home at night
and look my children in the eye. They see me as I am
anyway. To them I am the one who is away most of the day and who
talks softly to them at night and tosses them into the
air. Their thin faces come to me when I sleep and I try to
say as hard as I can "I love you" but all that happens is
that they turn away and run.

I'm not really sure who I work for its just a company name.
Most of the time, I just think of the foreman and my few
friends as the company and when we go for a drink after work
for a while I feel comfortable and full of power. When I get
home sometimes the children are already in bed. They both
look so hopeful when I look in on them I want to cry. Yet
late at night when one of them cries because of a bad dream,
I lie there and listen to them and just can't move. Later
in the morning when my wife asks if I heard them cry I lie.

I'm not sure she believes but she doesn't say anything. Sometimes I swear I am going to go mad but it never happens. Sometimes I wish it would happen so I could crawl inside myself for good. Then I think of my kids and my father and I know I'll be as sane as a him all my life. On those nights I dream of work I turn towards my wife and hold her as I tight as I can without waking her. In the morning I can tell that I did wake her after all just in the way she stumbles around the house. We never speak about such things I just give her a pat as I head off to the factory trying as hard as I can to shield my eyes from the glare of the sunlight.

TO HIM

To him there is no way out he has to stay to the
end not to watch but to be there to feel it when
she stops breathing. For some reason he thinks of
all those summer days drinking milkshakes and
dangling his feet in the water and thinking about
nothing in particular except maybe how he could
get enough money to buy another milkshake.
Sometimes now he holds her glass and listens to
her throat gurgle and he is numb. He waits for her
to speak to him but she doesn't. She listens for
his words words he can't say. Instead all
he is capable of is a gesture or two his hand near
hers as a nurse brings in a dinner tray. He hasn't
really thought about dying until now and all he
can think of is the nurses here everyday moving to
the sides of the dying or dead then returning at
night to a lover or family not shaking but trying
to bear up the best they can making spaghetti for
supper bathing a child moving lips in the dark as
if speaking to the dead. His own house is
forgotten now his wife lying alone while he sits
here not wanting to move not able to face her body
when they are in bed alone. Nothing except a glass
of lemonade on the night table. Her arms searching
for him but he can't let them find him.
Invisible to everyone even himself only here with
his mother near dark with the lights out in this
small hospital room does he become visible again.

She does not notice right away that he is there
not until he speaks, not to her but to himself
moving his lips as he has seen others do.
Sometimes he tries to read books to her but she waves
for him to stop before he has gotten very far. His
skin can't seal his sweat in and instead he lets
it soil his shirt and pants before he does

71

anything about it. But its not from heat that he
sweats its from standing in a room without light
and hearing his mother wail as if caught in
flames. He watches the costumes that all those who
come and go wear but in all of them he sees
nothing that will make a difference.

He sits up all night in the dark kitchen just
staring out a window trying to see death
approaching. But there is nothing outside except a
few stray cats who fill his thoughts with their
howling. He feels at the mercy of something but he
can't name it can't hold or feel it just knows
that it is there and he waits because that is all
that the living can do and he hates that tears at
his hair when no one is around puts his fist
through imaginary walls climbs to the top of a
tall building hoping to escape.

Each morning he is back at the hospital waiting
for the doctor to make her rounds and he listens
to the nurses laugh down the hall as her bath
fills. He moves his hands through the lukewarm
water hoping to find another hand beneath the
surface. He drinks the tea that a nurse leaves and
watches two sea gulls mate in the eaves of the
hospital and he is fascinated by their tenderness
and how they can stop for a moment even if the
world can't stop or protect them and they let down
their guard and as he listens to them but does not
hear them he knows that it is a long way from here
to any other perch and he no longer wants to try
for anything. He holds his mother's hand and
watches, for what, he doesn't know but watch he
does. On one of these occasions there will be
something that he will see and he will be glad.

72

His dreams are no longer fixed by the borders of
day or night instead he stands in a glow and holds
his mother's hand and for now the pain is all that
he can expect all that his life contains. He goes to
the window and watches the gulls mating and he
can feel a cry form inside a cry he knows that he is
incapable of sounding. His eyes are no longer able
to penetrate hers and stay fixed on the birds instead
as he prays. He knows that on the other side of the
earth the heavens have opened a little but neither
he nor she will ever be able to reach it. What is
left on the ground here is all that they have
left. His tongue hides in his mouth as he speaks
to her from the window his arms beginning to
change into wings.

MEANDERING

We look for evil in what a god does.
It is only through us
that gods know a false thing.
But gods are false too we find
in their chest a cavity we fill
with mirrors and with thoughts
we don't mean.

Today the buses are on strike and it
is too cold to venture out.
Stranded I take my arm from the window
sill. My head is as big as a god's
and yet it is filled with a single thought
one I can't get rid of. It remains
even as I walk into the cold.
This thought grows into madness
or evil and I am a fool because I chose
it and now it fills everything
I find in my body's own truth.

Gods are numbers safe in our minds.
Not plucked from the sky at all
not more certain than we about how to talk
to a lover. Inside our mothers
we form our bodies from a blueprint
they pass delicately to us
in their blood. After birth
we learn the parts of ourselves that
are the least god-like. Those features
we have no say over but bear until death.
Everything came true as we lived it
our lives bound by a brutality
we hardly recognize in others.

Life is an orchestra unwrapping its music
without the interference of a conductor.
I see too that the good is good whether
it is named or not. Evil is what
proclaims the false as true.
My own fingers on your
thigh is proof that I am wrong.

FALLING ASLEEP

Falling asleep is easy when your
head is empty, when the baby
has stopped teething, when your head
is in an oven, when the clock
stops ticking near the bed,
when your face forms a twisted union
with itself, when undressed
you pass the mirror and see nothing
but darkness poring out, when you have
not yet woken from the night before.

Forget the speeches that cows dream into
your life, forget the anger of fish
near your bed, forget the lovers who pass
you and look away, forget the insane asylum
where you learned to sleep,
forget the mother who lost you in her arms,
forget your arm asleep, numb as a bruise,
forget the weight you are forced to bear but don't,
forget the loneliness that heaven promises,
forget the sky that is not there when you turn
but there anyway, small confused, as blue as a
bruise on the temple, forget the plants that
die over the winter, each spring their
stiff brown stalks refuse to fill with green, forget
how awkwardly you lifted yourself out of sleep
walking through a strange airport like a drunken terrorist.

Lie awake in bed until the vibrations of morning
are too much to ignore, or the neighbours start
to sing opera and you can feel the paint
peel above you, or the phone rings and you
think of a lover even though you know its a wrong number

or someone selling carpet cleaner, or the sky hypnotizes
you in the skylight, or the smell of coffee threatens you,
or you feel your heart blow up underneath its
bunker of flesh, or you feel your penis crawl between
your legs slowly like a snail fleeing a fire, or
you need to pee and can't hold it any longer as the
sun balances in intimidation directly above you, or
looking around the room you see what night has deposited
on the furniture, or you need to look in the mirror
to see if faces last longer than one night.

GOD IS THE SMALLEST OBJECT

God is the smallest object in a room. Some of us
see it and speak to it as if it were a pet or a
lover. Others imagine it was bigger and could not
fit into this room at all. Others still fall in
love with it and take it to bed with them every
night. Some of us can't even get into the room at
all and must stare at the object from the doorway
like a prisoner staring at the sea from their cell
window. This object does not move or breathe or
even love. It merely thinks about ways to get out
of this room for good. It thinks about wings about
legs about fingers but none of them is adequate.
In the end this object decides that it is stuck
for good in this room. Those that truly love it
will pick it up and throw it out the window. Those
who despise it will try to hide it beneath some
large piece of furniture. Most of us however will
take no notice of it merely sitting next to it
once in a while and glancing at it from the corner
of our eyes hoping that sometime we will discover
what to do with it.

BEAUTIFUL ACCIDENTS

My country has no blood but it bleeds each day and as I
wander under its many skies I can feel the blood on my
fingers and can taste it behind my teeth. Each morning I
pick a rose from my garden and wear it in my lapel and I
feel old in this country of mine where the flowers
always seem to fall asleep in your hand where the birds
wait on stumps for the faint hint of sulphur to leave
the air. In this country of mine I am neither a woman
nor a man neither bird nor flower merely the one who
adds the sounds that those who pass hear. I smell the
dead as they weave their tender path through the earth.
In my country I build houses, streets, roads, schools
everything I need except a lover. No arm or tongue is
available there is nothing but beautiful accidents that
make me think of you alone in your country too walking
across its lush green pastures as if looking for a place
where the earth will let you be. Beneath my country the
earth sags: the lakes seep into one another. I am half
crazy with trying to find beauty as if it were something
that could be noticed in all the junk around me. Angels
camp on the west borders of my country and I do not
notice do not care because their patience tires me as I
look in their direction and imagine that they interpret
my country as a lover interprets a heaving blanket. I am
not noble or perfect in my country I am merely someone
who stands on the hillside and watches as something
green claims the valley each spring.

ISABEL

I think of Isabel
and her quiet eyes
not yet seeing the light
that poisons everything.
She moves a finger to an eye
and rubs it as if trying
to change its colour or what it saw.
When she speaks she stands
straight moving her hands as if
they could keep her from lying.

When I take one of her hands,
she whispers and I listen.
She grew around the violence
in her life as if it could be
cured by her flesh.
She discovered in Canada
that evil does not stop when you move
to another place it changes.
What comes apart can't just be patched
Can't just be loved
a different way. No it is lost.
Gone. Claimed by something neither
greater nor less just something that
holds a place in everything.

Isabel speaks to me now though
she is dead. There are rooms
in my house where she has left a scent
or a finger print. But I do not
look for that. I remember
her with an apple round and red
in her hand
happy as if violence
was something you could leave behind
like furniture. I never once looked

through her eyes or found the window
she was looking for. But neither did she.
He killed her and the baby
and then himself and only he was happy.
Some days I stop before their house
just blocks from mine and I try
to hear some sound she might have left
for me. Each car that passes
as I stand on her street I imagine
the driver holding a pistol in his left
hand as he drives by just as he did
that last day parking in front of her
house as if he was on a friendly visit.
He hid the gun in his pocket like
a bag of candy or a handkerchief.

Even to the end you hoped he would change
that all the evil was left behind you.
I could have told you there is
no paradise but would you have listened?
Would I have been right?
The street where you lived has
changed. Your house has changed.
Others have come to claim its rooms
for themselves. Sometimes as I pass
I see one of them standing
at the door just as confused as I am.
The doctor who treated you when
your husband burned your hands is my doctor
but we never speak of you
as if you were a secret that
we had to keep to ourselves.

Some days my daughter asks about you
and I tell her that you have moved
to another city. She asks me to describe it
for her. I take her hand and kiss it
and she smiles and soon forgets
that her father has not answered her.
I fear most the violence that I keep
from her. Locked inside me.
When she says your name, Isabel,
I want to kiss her. I want to
find a wound on her skin and heal it.
My wife still carries your picture
in her wallet. I have seen her take it
out now and then when she is looking for something.
As your lost eyes are struck by the light
once again, I must turn away and protest
everything I know.

Sometimes when my wife appears
in the door she wears a black halo
just like everyone else did that day.
I covered mine with a hat when I went out.

OUR MOTHERS HIDE US

Our mothers hide us in their bodies
claiming each day a little bigger space
for us. We fit perfectly inside them
and are disguised by a film of water.
Our eyes are blind and
our fingers are joined together.
We ask our mothers how it is out there
and how our fathers look as they stand before
mirrors parting their hair. Our mothers
answer not with words or sounds but
by moving their hands to their bellies.

Our mothers have hidden us and we do
not understand why until much later
when as parents ourselves we see
that there is a coldness that bodies
can lapse into. We earn nothing
in these few hours we live nothing
except the size of a mother's love.
Whole lifetimes are spanned in a week.
We find the killing and the animals we
used to be in words in books reading
them as our lives hiss around us
no longer saved by a body or made whole
by a mother's warm hand.
Our own children are not pure
do not save the world do not
find again the high places that were lost.
We enjoy their smiles the small faces
they examine everything with.
As parents we examine photographs
and learn the will behind all things.
The faint glimmering that
fills a mother's final act.

CRUEL SUN

Father and son translate the world slowly intensifying
each element of it with their own grief and joy. The next
doctor in a long line of doctors will notice something but
it will be too late and all that is known will be
stupefied and written in English for convenience. They
are careful with the magnificence of being father and son
now nothing else matters except the light over the other's
shoulder. Each doctor does the same speaks first to the son
then to the father reversing the familiar order of being. The father
knows that sometime he is going to have to ask his
son to leave the room. He dresses fastidiously each day and
what he covers is his own decaying: the white cold flesh.
The son drives in from the suburbs each evening to find his father.

Near one corner of the room old boots rest. The father
occasionally plays the piano when the son visits and music
amplifies the fading. The father's face is peaceful. Each
moment a delicate echo of what has gone before. Afterwards
from his worn bed he watches his son leave and counts his
footsteps listening for the falter on the last step.

Last month on the way home from the clinic the father
spoke of dying as if it were just another town he plans to
visit. The son did not listen turned to his father and
smiled and moved his body as though he had a sudden itch.
Today each word is chosen as if to erase the one before
it. By graceful degrees they find what they have lost all
those years ago. The father plays his death gently pausing
to linger yet one more hour in a memory that never was.
He faces the equations that the son ignores knows
that everything can be found in the hollow light.
He pursues everything and nothing enjoys his son's
visits but never lets on careful to plan his remaining
time as he has done his whole life. He smokes a
cigarette and regrets nothing. The mouth the hardest thing
to close in the end.

TREES

Trees cover the earth with their noises
and still we do not hear them.
We lie in bed while the slaughter continues
and we feel nothing. Death passes
through us and we do not shiver.
Tree roots reach into the darkness
of the earth and find what our hearts can not.
Even the roots of toppled trees continue
to struggle through the dirt aimless.
While we pave over everything with little
guilt. Trees dance as they die and
we wait in a cool November chill watching
as each tree sinks slowly to the ground.
Then white or red flesh is cut open
and still we do not stop our work long
enough to feel the trees' quick death.
Nothing waits for us now but a cold bed
our bodies no longer able to warm themselves.
Our eyes no longer able to stop
the sunlight's subversion.

Trees comfort the dead cradle them
with their loving roots
while we wait at home to heal and
sit in our backyards feeling the
wind across our rough faces.
The dead have too many rules we think
and do not bother to listen to them
when we visit the small places in
the ground we have marked with their names.
Who will hear us when we are gone
we ask and know the answer is no one
we will be the last to go left

in a crumbling house the streets filled
with a few wandering weeds and the moon
so yellow we think it is the sun.

Perhaps it is too late now to do anything
but let our bodies slip slowly into death.
Our lovers going first their eyes suddenly
filled. In death their feet will look like roots
as we uncover them.

JESUS

Space is boundless inside a god's head
and it is impossible to say what echoes
linger there. Jesus was crucified because
he noticed things. He noticed how inside
a god's head there wasn't room for any
truth except continuance of light.
Shadows fell across Jesus' face as he
wept high above the crowd. Later he
slept through the end, his eyes aimed
at the ground not the sky. He knew that
History would take a long time to
bend the light away from his face.
Then he was overcome with the beauty
a soul finds as it dies. He imagined gods
kissing his hand, angels sweetening the air
with their breaths. He heard all the horrors
in the world sucked into a single melody
a sound so joyous even the most doubtful
would have been filled with it.
His body slipped from him then and he learned
to approximate its shape although it was gone.
He thought of the diseases that gods gently
pass on. He thought of the deaths that would come
He thought of his feet dangling
in the blood water of soldiers raiding adjoining houses.
Becoming a god means losing the moment.

Jesus began his life over: first as a thief,
roaming the streets lured by the scent of the old, the lame.
He learned the rules from the beautiful and the weary.
Later he returned to the cross, tired of letting
his eyes lift him upwards. Then he became a king.
Slept with his back to the wall. All night he would
not attempt to open his eyes. By morning
he could feel his hands begin to dry. During the day
he would move through the crowds as though searching

for the one face that could free him. He never found it
or learned the names of any of those who passed him
in great numbers everyday. He discovered the loneliness
of power, and the rage that goes with it. Learned
that even the tongue can stop its dancing if it is willed.
At night he returned to the cross to feel the earth
close as he climbed back to his suffering.
Our gods suffer to learn how hard
we are to love. His days of pain
help us to feel a god's tenderness is not enough.
Jesus offered a warning, came each night to our side
and listened as our sleep poured out.
He watched as our limbs twitched to a imperceptible rhythm.
We are the ones, not him, that accept the excuses and stand
at a window as though offering a sniper a chance.
Our bodies are satisfied by the warm flesh of eggs.
Our spirits linger in the darkness of morning.
We tell ourselves a god didn't bring us this far
our debts are only to ourselves, to the lingering
of our breaths in the air. Through the fire Jesus
comes lightless and free. He has suffered too
long for us and now he is free. He doesn't stare
as he passes he just nods and laughs as history tries
to follow him from room to room. We watch as he moves
gracefully through the crowd. Stopping now and
then to fill a glass or to look into the eyes
of someone. His feet glide softly across the marble.
Suddenly he begins to whistle and everyone turns
around. We grow to hate him and to underestimate his
desire to be rid of us. After a while
we check our own breathing noting that even it
has begun to change. Slowly we undress as Jesus
stands once more on the cross. Small and plastic now
he hangs above our bed and listens each night as
we empty ourselves with sleep. In the morning
we wear the sunlight like a coat we want to show off.